10/26/01

Marion,

Best wishes!

Mel Belin

FLESH THAT WAS CHRYSALIS

by Mel Belin

THE WORD WORKS
CAPITAL COLLECTION

First Edition
First Printing
Flesh That Was Chrysalis

Book design, typography: Janice Olson
Cover art: *Romance,* by Noi Volkov, 1997, oil on canvas, 37" by 47"
Production management: Marta Levcheva
Printed in Bulgaria

Library of Congress Number: 98-60612
International Standard Book Number: 0-915380-40-4

Acknowledgments

Acknowledgment is made to the following publications in which some of the poems in this book appeared originally in the current, or occasionally, in an earlier version: *Antietam Review*, "Because He Didn't Ask For Directions"; *Blue Unicorn*, "Thrush And Flux"; *The Cape Rock*, "Anniversary," "Early March In The Park," and "Shoe Shine Man"; *Connecticut River Review*, "Leaf and Tree"; *Gryphon*, "Patriarch"; *Cumberland Review*, "A Visit"; *Jewish Spectator*, "From The Psychoanalysis Of A Sodomite Juggler" and "Isaac's Weaning Feast"; *Karamu*, "Homecoming"; *The Lyric*, "Juggler"; *Midstream*, "Eden"; *Phoebe*, "ira," and "Vision"; *Poet Lore*, "Pas De Deux"; *Potomac Review*, "Cosmic Law," "Dawn After Reading *The Magus* Together," "Mandolin And Shroud," and "The Rogue Swans That Like Classical Music"; *Response: A Contemporary Jewish Journal*, "Flesh That Was Chrysalis"; *South Coast Poetry Journal*, "Jael"; *Visions*, "The Mephisto Waltz"; and *Wind*, "Audrey Rose." The poem "Vision," noted above, also was published in an anthology by the Washington Writers Publishing House, entitled *Hungry as we are* (1995). The poem, "The Rogue Swans That Like Classical Music," was winner of *The Potomac Review's* third annual poetry competition. "Cosmic Law" and "Dawn After Reading *The Magus* Together" were both finalists in earlier *Potomac Review* poetry competitions. "Because He Didn't Ask For Directions," was a runner-up in *Antietam Review's* 1998 poetry competition. Special thanks to Don Franck, Ronnie Wainwright and the New Room Poets for their critical help with this book.

Table of Contents

WEBS

COSMIC LAW

In loving memory of my parents,
Sol and Beatrice Belin

Juggler

He is a juggler. Up into the air—
one ball, two balls, three. The entire show
is spinning through his hands. He does not know
how long to play the game. He does not care.
He plays it day and night, and with a prayer
he keeps it going even though the snow
has started falling softly, even though
the bombs are falling. There is no despair.
He is a juggler. One ball, two balls, three.
And as he tosses, nations rise and fall.
Under a Torquemada men may bend
or break. Then in a flash they're standing free
and tall. For centuries, he's seen it all.
He juggles balls.
He'll be here in the end.

Pass Over

Homecoming

I put an ear to the glowing wall,
listen quietly.
There's action in the pumping chamber
where blood is sent spurting out.
Sixteen years.
Quite a spell to have been
away.
                Looming above: a wrap-
around front and side porch;
yellow shingles. Inside, a confusion
of rooms: some large and airy;
others like collapsed accordions—
secret places.
                                        A voice, both shriek
and song, drew me across hundreds of miles
to this: Mother, hair chestnut young,
trembling to let me in. Her steps draw near.
Father waits in the soft gemütlich leather
of his chair. The children at play:
Brother and myself.
                                                        On the tongue, words dis-
assemble. I look over and through the peeling
paint, cracked windows, see the place
as I think it was. Not real, but so bright
the eyes hurt. Like staring at the sun too long.
When the door opens, I can't see to enter.

Patriarch

I had a stake. That's why I should've been
with you when you were left behind without
a passport in Mogilev, where horses
pulled the trolleys on long thin rails and peasants
carted in loads of freshly chopped wood.

In the starless pitch and bite of winter,
I see myself ride the jolting wagon
to the border, your mouth smoking vapor.
You pat the horse goodby. "Wait! I'm
coming!" I cry, chasing after you

through the woods, every nocturnal sound
amplified unnaturally. Later, upon slipping
into Latvia, when you're cornered
on the synagogue roof: I warn "They carry
guns. Be careful!" as you move to the ledge, leap

for me, even though you don't know it,
the pavement exploding upwards,
on your way to Riga, Libava,
an Ellis Island reunion with your parents,
long before I was born.

Great-grandma Minnie

Only once did we meet.
You reached out, bones going click and creak
from the home of a bed.
"Come here, little one!"
I was hugged *in extremis.*
Far below,
the world flew by—bicycles, cars
in a park thick leafy green,
bells that tugged,
the *Good Humor Man's.* You drew me
back—does he know Hebrew? To the light
of your face I chanted: *"Baruch*
atah Adonai . . ."
And though I didn't see
the shtetl girl throwing snow
at a dray horse,
or on Siegel Street, the sheen—
ice jewels—that hung by the cornice
of your house, couldn't see anything
for that matter save the light,
it brought its own spell.
"Will he
be bar mitzvahed?" you asked.
Mother nodded.
Years from then, I learned
how you had sat in that house,
fashioned dresses, scarves
in puce, lavender, ocher for six daughters until—
mazel tov, finally—Irving.
As an adult, he'd pick you up,

play dervish spinning around.
His little game!
Face flushed, you'd cry: *"Gottenyu,* stop!"
And when he did—
walls, lamps, tables awhirl in the head,
you both laughed.
                    One day he coughed
blood.
He hugged you as you did me when we said
goodby. I was pulling away . . .
You drew me back, lips moving, though barely
a sound, not ready to let go, rocked with me
only seconds, half croon, half whisper now,
"Az du mayn kind, vest elter vern . . ."
("When my little baby's grown . . ."), your arms
trembling on the edge of the bed.

Stevensville

That summer in the Catskills, peeping out
behind grapefruit, green olives,
bouillon *en tasse,* roast Philadelphia caponette,
potato pudding, Hungarian apple strudel—

more food. On Swan Lake, I try to row it off.
Then shag flies with my *Wally Moon* special,
a glove with a pocket so small
I never know if I'm to blame for the balls
that pop out of it.

Each day we grow plumper,
till I see the dishes in dreams: gefilte fish,
chicken broth with kasha, young pullet
jardinière, honey cake. My name
has roots of honey from the Latin *mel*
and means in Gaelic "polished chief,"

but when my older brother taunts me about it
in a mincing falsetto,
I want to kill or disappear.
Father warns: "you have to learn how to take it,"
paints a picture of the world—a lifetime
of frustration with it, austere too,

like the garb of the Chassidim, whom I'd never seen
until the trip here, with their twisting earlocks,
even the youngsters. "Hey, look at that,"
he'd called out when we passed through Monticello,
a puckish smile and disapproval co-joined,
as if in America *they* should be like the rest

of *us.* Last dinner: Lake Erie pike *en aspic,*
matzah dumpling consommé,
broiled beef flanken with potato *boulangère,*
radish rosettes, carrots *vichy,*
raspberry *linzer* tortes. I waddle away
from the table like a lurching top.

A Visit

He lies in bed like a toadstool uprooted,
tubes everywhere. "It's nice to see my boyala,"
he says. *I used to tag along with him to work.*
I'd collect spools of thread and sort them
by color—chartreuse, magenta, crimson.

The blood drains into him from a sack,
perched overhead like a bobbin.
"I came because . . ."—he wouldn't talk
on the phone. I juggled plans, caught
the Miami flight. *When he needed me,*

he'd flush me out from between jacket parts,
pockets, trousers in the upper levels of huge
storage bins. *"This is discouraging,"* he says;
and I want to unhook him, drive him away . . .
"Son! How about a ride in the pushcart?"

I roll past whirring sewers down a steep incline
into the basement where cutters slice through
layers of cloth. I dismount to watch them.
"Come here, fella!" It's Carmen, the presser,
face sopping, huge stains on his undershirt.

"Your father's quite a man. He's the boss!"
"Yes, I know," I say, as if I know everything.
The nurses hover with their charts and needles.
"Give me your arm!" one of them orders.
"Show him how the boss does it!" Carmen urges.

Dad lifts the big hot iron with a facile
gesture, plunks it smartly across the seat
of a skirt, sizzling away the creases.
The drawing of blood. Puffs of steam rise
to the ceiling. The tube fills up crimson.

Early March In The Park

Light as the Frisbee's curl and glide,
this day when everything calls,
from the whistled *whooee*
of a starling high on sun to the guitar's
strum in this noontide's pulse
and throb. The tessellated
tables for chess are alive. The stone-cut
nymph, naked save for a fluttering
cloth, is alive. She props up,
like a caryatid, in the humming warmth, a huge
fountain. A profusion of people spill
over the benches, onto the grass.
The bearded man, flask stashed in a paper bag,
doesn't need a lick, with a smile, lost
and found, like the children
who play-wrestle or the black girl with a purple
balloon. The drifting newspaper is alive.
The can of Coke, the piece of glass
are alive. Each in its own way reaches, like the petals
of flowers sheathed underground, for the sun.
My grandmother calls me with a hug.
I haven't seen her in the twenty years since
she died. She's brought me hard boiled eggs
and a tomato. We sit by the fountain
the stone-cut nymph lifts higher. Waters shoot and spray.

Players

I'm getting spooked waiting for Sunday.
A babble of voices contend.
The Jew rises up, invokes Hitler.
She's Catholic, he accuses.
The lawyer intercedes. It's not hopeless,
though negotiations would be needed
over the children. Who's talking
marriage? snarls the hedonist. I hardly
know her. The spiritualist crunches
into a half-lotus, meditates, only
to have the poet shoulder the mantra
aside. He wonders if there's a poem
in the ginkgo trees she's talked about, still
sporting fan-shaped yellow leaves in December.
Interesting, says the nascent botanist.
The neurotic worries. So many things
can go wrong, like bumping into someone,
dropping a dish, stumbling for everyone
to laugh, oh boy, tears streaming from the eyes:
there goes that fella who can't find love. He's
a loner. He is: pouring over dusty tomes,
writing his heart out, the sap, just to see
the words on paper, 'cause no one else gives
a damn. The little boy, rejected by his
brother, wants a friend, reaches for the child
whose parents divorced, her punishment, she thinks,
for unknown sins. Let's go and play, he says.
Then there are the lovers, macho man
and the sensitive male. Her earth mother
and feminist sidekicks pace the sidelines.
I'm getting spooked waiting for Sunday.
Our players troop forward, coachless. The trees
drop their leaves, reach out with naked arms.

Dawn After Reading *The Magus* Together

The sun has not yet risen. Jetty stones
are wet with nighttime and a surge of spray
that stops us halfway out.
                                        The morning groans
awake fitfully here on Cape May.

We sit and hug the chilly air away,
as clean and mindless as the empty shore,
a giant lighthouse piercing through the grey
nothingness.

                        Peignoir rucked up on the floor,
your long bare thighs evoke in their motion
an urgency as of the huntress'
                                                    cries,
the thrash of the tide.
                                    We are no longer
ourselves, moorings unloosed, cast off,
                                                            your moan,
salt-water deep: the current carries
us wordlessly to a threshold
                                                and over

The Rogue Swans That Like Classical Music

They flew onto the woman's lawn,
ten, twenty, forty . . . , grabbed their spots
on the grassy embankment even as the last
movement of Beethoven's Ninth—*Freude, schöner*
Götterfunken . . . blaring from the speakers—
started to lift off. Transfixed,
something in their avian brains
had caught: not the words themselves,
but the spell, "Joy, bright spark of divinity . . ."
This is the mute swan, *Cygnus olor,*
with roots, old world Eurasian,
under attack now by environmentalists,
who complain how it over-
consumes, pollutes, proliferates.
They've had their eggs shaken
to scramble embryos. Wings pinioned.
Guns aimed at . . . And though they may look
immaculate in form, a feathery white to bring snow
to summer, they are not (is this not the swan
that ravished poor Leda?) pure
as all that downy show.
And yet having gathered now,
as if by right,
as if patrician and with season tickets,
they are like the ethereal
rush of this music, ageless,
in the morning light,
the old world rising, its great wing beats.

When All The Doors Of The World Are Shut

Into the turning lane,
past the beggar with a scrawled sign
"lost my wife and job," up the ramp
to the mall, where he parks
the car, leaves his key—closing
the door—in the ignition
behind. O my God! He calls

AAA. No answer. What the hell
are they doing there? He hails a cab
home. Alas, when he arrives,
the Condo Office has just closed, no chance
to get their backup key (his home key
is on the chain in the car) to open
his apartment where lying in a drawer
is a second car key. But wait!

If he hails a cab to take him to work,
there's a key to his apartment
there . . . And then doing just that,
he remembers he doesn't have his work ID,
or the key to the door of his office, feels
in that instant what it must be like, the un-
raveling, when all the doors of the world

are shut. Soon, though, he will persuade
security to help him get the key
that gets the key that gets
the key . . . And oh, the bliss of finally
driving his car out of the mall—
there's the beggar, still out in the heat;
he'll stare past him—onto the main
drag, step on the gas and forget.

Blackie

A dog called Blackie, yelping his hellos—
Here boy! Down boy!—in that yard-front, possessed.
Sniffing at the fence. Then up at the snows
falling silently.
                                        So many years pressed
into a daguerreotype of that time.

A child's nose flush against the window—
mine—, a squall line, like a tide, swirling in
a pseudo-dusk.
                                        Then there's the undertow
that swept us reeling out to the future.

Transfixed by images that overlay—
what *is* and *was*—back to aeons before
that dog and boy, sculpt of primal clay
from the kiln of stars . . .
                                                        Another winter,
brrrr the lost self, snow swallowing day.

Breakfast

with an existential biscuit

The morning after Ralph Kramden takes
dance lessons to learn the Hucklebuck,
I breakfast at *Roy Rogers*. I come because

it's going out of business, even as I collect
old TV shows. Why can't I let
go? I enjoy sitting across from the huge

plate glass windows, with the words
"OREO" and "SHAKE," backwards
from the inside—their mirror image, that is—

like to watch it snow—how the wind
picks up the flakes and sends them scurrying
across the pane: hoods are tightened,

heads bow down. The same old man today,
his hair a wispy white, with his Bible
and coffee has been here every time

I am, for the last ten years—
a modern day malady, that we never say
hello. At night, I curl up on my sofa,

like a cat on a warm stove, laughing
as Ralph goes roller-skating
with Alice, ends up on his prodigious

butt. The next day, I savor my favorite
"cinnamon 'n' raisin" biscuit with tea.
A new clientele here, a horde of homeless

with their plastic bags and smell.
I don't care: annihilation of what doesn't
interest us creates its own reality.

Thrush And Flux

A winter field, browns
and yellows to a slate grey
horizon. In the middle
of plucked cornstalks,
hunched on top of one, a peep
of blue. Who really sees
whom? The traveler who's
stopped by the roadside,
or this iris of the field
that stares back? Almost as
eyes lock, mind enmeshing
mind, they slip past
each other. The bluebird
darts off for berries.
No katydids or beetles
this day. The car rolls
away. Later, crows attack
a sharp-shinned hawk
above woods and shivering
Choptank. Snows start up,
every flake an eye that,
for a moment, sees us.

Celebration At Mallory Square

After a day of clouds and rain,
they must have known something I didn't
here in Key West's Mallory Square:
the clown whose dog,
dressed in a farcical skirt
hopped down from atop a ladder
to snatch a dollar
out of a boy's teeth;
or the Russian emigré,
one moment thumping his chest,
the next balancing a stove
from his mouth.
                    Had Mr. Yogi
who lay on a bed of nails
seen this happen before?
When as he'd asked,
a woman dropped a bowling ball, ouch!
on his chest, he had a beatific look . . .
It was as unexpected
as the little girl, who smiled
with a fourteen foot Burmese python
wrapping around her, its tongue
slithering.
              And for the first time that day,
through a rent in the clouds,
the sun above the horizon
peeked—as if it liked what it saw,
came out fully! Maybe it's like being
old before one learns to live,
how it doesn't matter, nothing
matters, only such
a moment triumphant, blood-red—
mere wisps of clouds across
its face, the inconsequence
of what had been.

Seder

"And I will harden Pharaoh's heart . . ."
Exodus, 7.3

Lamb's blood on the door.
Moloch-ha-Movis,
Angel of Death.
Pass over.

A cup of wine for Elijah.
The door left open
a crack. Welcome.
Come in.

People of flesh.
We have been chosen.
Transfigured.
Dip

parsley in salt water—
the sea, mother
of life, its arms,
opening

wide—a holy miracle—
to let us through.
People of spirit
brought

low. Take
the bitter herbs now!
Naked in the pit
for slaves—

before Christ, relativity,
the ego, the id.
What is it we built?
Pyramids.

Brought
low, toiling in
the mud; yet still
they stand—

soaring stone, a tomb,
a dream, monuments
to what dark part
of ourselves?

From the clay
of earth . . . Above
skies. We celebrate
freedom.

Matzoh to share
and songs.
Freedom! With lamb's
blood

on the door.
A cup of wine for Elijah.
Why is this night different?
Pass over. Come in.

Mandolin And Shroud

"I played 'Csardas' by Monti,
in all of the clubs,"
he'd said, sitting in the wheelchair.
Voice rising, "Oh, how I played, from Riga
to Brooklyn," and his legs,
tumor-swollen, looked like they wanted
to dance.
He hummed a tune,
but what stayed: how he stepped
out of a cab near the el, left
his mandolin behind; and as the driver
spun away to the din of a train passing,
his life switched
tracks. A moment,
precise as the machines
he worked with in the Navy Yard. Never
played a note again. He got married,
had children. Later, he owned
a factory.
Now at ninety, re-
discovering art, he's crafting a poem
about himself. Face pinched
bone-white, he begins to read
haltingly: "Money money money,
an old story . . ."
On a day he feels
better, he adds: "It may not be so sad,
and not as bad," though a home for the aged
still has him swallowing hard,
"the snake pit's for me when it suits
my family."
For months, he's been like this,
knits words together as if he were
fashioning a shroud, but shrinks
from finishing. "The piece will change,"
he promises, "as I change." It hurts him to write,
as it does to move his legs. And not to.

The Great Smoked Whitefish

On the trail, eyes growing wide
with some gustatory memory
from years ago, smacking his lips,
kissing his fingers; he'd been wasting away—
the cancer; no appetite—
though he blamed his daughter-in-law.
Her meatballs were hard,
the chicken dry. Was she trying
to kill him? he'd asked.
But once out of the wheelchair

into the car, he forgot her, forgot
his dream, too, of the starving birds
and cats—odd, because he owned none.
"Innocent pets," he'd said, "it was sad,
and then . . ." voice exuberant:
"Someone new took them in who loved
and fed them. Oh how happy they became;
they kissed the hands of the owners
who fed them." Sunroof open, he relaxed
as we drove. And soon we'd taken off,

air streaming, the Hebrew music in the car—
Hevenu Shalom . . . , Hava Nagila,
Zemer, Zemer, Lach, and many more.
He exclaimed, louder each time,
"hey, Hey, HEy," clapped too, heart
leaping with the beat of the song.
How far, it seemed, from a week before—
or was it later?—when he'd said, "Inevitable
is a word that's strong; I don't think
I'll last . . ." His voice had quavered. I cut

it off in myself, not wanting to hear.
The leaves, crimson, orange, gold; we tried
Stop And Shop in Cromwell, Middletown . . .
No luck. With a wave of the hand, he urged us
on. The trees flared at the bottom
of the hill! And then upward, the day growing
thin. Quicksilver. Darting with colors
as we reached higher. At *Waldbaum's,* a catch:
huge. Filling the car with the glitter of scales.
"Inevitable . . . ." From out of the depths

to this heartland: smoked flesh, mythic.
He explained, "you cut off the head first,
then the tail," his hand in short, abrupt slices.
Filling the day! In the wind, leaves; dazzle
of memories; light. Trembling. Like an aspic.
Soft. Unexpected. And beyond the shell of his body—
shriveled, crippled—he grasped the fish. Raced
with it up the stoop to brothers sisters Father
Mother arms open wide, welcoming. Soon
they would feast as with something holy.

Flood

The dream was of a flood. We were
back in the shtetl, which was being washed
away: Father and I, that is.
He'd grabbed a battered suitcase

and started to stuff it with shirts, ties,
dollars. His face was drawn and white.
He's dying, they'd said of him: osteoblastic
changes, *progressive.* A good word, turned bad.

"C'mon, he said, let's run," as if we could
do it together, outstep cancer. His dream
of the shtetl, not mine. To his parting
"Drive care-ful-ly!" (as if I were

endangered too): I reached for a suitcase
(battered), the week's visit over. His oncologist,
who gave him six months (three years ago),
he'd dubbed the *Moloch ha Movis* ("Angel

of Death"). On the long ride home, leaving . . .
through the splatter of rain and fog
by the Tappan Zee bridge, the windshield wipers
going click click; further to the south,

the Garden State Parkway, and the succession
of tolls you must pay to pass. Leaving.
Every month he'd visit the *Moloch,* as he called
him for short. He'd say it lightly sometimes,

his joke, zip up his lips, deadpan, mutter
through the pain, "he's not controversial,"
muddling words. He meant "conversational."
Dr. Brown, a quiet man in a white jacket,

but with wings too; he can take off . . . fly.
I could barely see through the downpour
on the turnpike south, jammed on brakes
to avert a crash. Night in midday. I wanted

to turn back: to a milkcan in the newly
flowing river, shingles stripped from peasant
hovels. But it was too late! From an upper story
window, a woman in a babushka cried.

Flesh That Was Chrysalis

Eden

"(T)hese things were in the Garden Of Eden
on Earth, but all were shaped . . . after . . .
things . . . in the supernal Garden Of Eden."
Kabbala, Bahya ben Asher, Biur 'al haTora 1:67-69

Feathers hum in the wind.
Splash of green, long black tail—
the tiny bird darts from drooping catkins
to blossom clusters bright like suns. In the distance,
spirits of the righteous elude demon hordes
led by the Sword of Ashmodai the King, face aflame,
and visions of Samael riding a serpent like a camel
on the road to

Eden. The ground here,
every bush and flower too, have beads of dew
that resurrect the dead. Then there are
the thousand palaces of longing where the Messiah
dwells. Once when he saw a woman crying, a teardrop
burnt down his face. The Garden
world quaked.

The hummingbird fluttering
one moment, the next . . .
gone. The Garden, too. A crack
across the world, tremorous,
widening:
a gorge, a chasm uncrossable.

Lilith

Face flushed, breasts heaving, she flaps her wings
through the moonlit casement into a man's flat
millennia after that first rejection. Darkness' avatar
flashing jewels like stars! How many fools have kissed her
on such visits? First female, tangled in bedsheets
before there was such a thing. Eve was still
an unsuspecting rib when this nubile princess
could have become mother of us all, had Adam
wrapped around her pinky, save for an act before
its time. Now she travels with a crowd who don't
begrudge her the top—Samael, Qaftzefoni,
Ashmodai. But it's mortals she's driven to ride
to gates that guard the dragon, and then, inside.

Flesh That Was Chrysalis

Skin prickling strangely, he closes
his eyes. Desire, unearthly, pulls
at him; suddenly the darkness explodes
with what he mistakes
for rage. His Age is one of debauchery;
and he, Enoch, a living oddity, born
circumcised. He's sprouting
wings!
          Ten . . . (The earth
recedes). Thirty . . . yet, still, more keep
coming out. Terror, unimaginable;
and then transmuted, he hurls himself higher,
each wing, a whole world,
                              and a myriad of eyes,
like stars. The angels blink
back from this flambeau of flesh, complain:
What is this smell of a woman born?
How he can see past them now . . .
toward places never before imagined: he soars
through seven heavens to the highest
                                        for his Imago.
Reaching, he becomes it.
                              He's called Jahoel,
Prince of the Face, and most commonly
Metatron from the Greek, *metadronos,*
he who pursues with vengeance,
and *meta ton thronon,* nearest

to the Divine throne:
                         he who if permitted
by the Holy One
could create a universe
with planets, black holes and quasars,
once sat beside a tamarisk munching figs.

From The Psychoanalysis Of A Sodomite Juggler

Don't look back, I said in the dream,
as if I could save her, not knowing from what.
Surely not the jackal's carcass rotting on the path
behind! Only when *it* metamorphosed into our unblessed
city—ramparts, towers, and all—even as earth
opened jaws beneath, expired sulfurous fumes—
Oh, *God,* I mumbled (not having used the word
before made it seem more unreal) —fire and brimstone
swirling down. A thought—the soothsayer *did* call

for showers . . .—when I, in mid-life
crisis, a deformed leg to boot, saw her (she's the only one
who didn't laugh). Arms outstretched, burbling
with pleasure, I enfolded her to me de-li-cate-ly,
uncovered moments later . . . a mangy pillow. Her phantom
from the twilight edges of the room, and echoes of past
times together—dreamed/real?—mocked me.
I've juggled stones, pomegranates, men, animals—
my sexual proclivities are wide—now this pulchritudinous . . .

Doctor, when I awoke, lusting so much that my hands—livelihood—
trembled in the balance, the act was past the point of no
return, husband-cum-cuckold notwithstanding. I skedaddled out
of the city towards you in Zoar because I had to talk,
though for too many shekels an hour. You're frowning.
No, I'm not passive-aggressive . . . A day later,
(Stop shaking the head!) just like in the dream,
(Forget the aside already!) this you can't deny:
a cataclysm of such dimension, the sky a dark, pendulous

horror, and my lover, a pillar—you've got to believe me,
she's disappeared—of salt. Such earthiness there.
I sprinkle, savor her with every edible morsel . . . Yes, salt
with an s. S-a-l-t! I may be, instead of sublimating . . .
Obsessive-compulsive, you say? No, hypertensive!
I'm glad you *see* the problem. Also, the men who *craved* me
for what would make any Sodomite proud are all gone. As for Lot,
he's been—I've heard it in the best of circles—sleeping
with his daughters. *They* need help too! What's a fella to do?

Isaac's Weaning Feast

Milling about. Ubiquitous moon-smiles,
as hands reach for fatted calf, honey cakes,
an assortment of sweet fruits. The target, Sarah,
the nonagenarian who'd proclaimed herself
the foundling's *real* mother. Yuk-yuk! between
bites, and swills from *good stuff,* not rotgut.

Present, a *who's who* for Kadesh and Shur.
Lots of tots too, dangling from elbows,
gurgling on laps, cushions. Dancers
command a circle of clappers by the terebinths.
A pageant of hips that sway, taut thighs
beneath fluted skirts, the tambourine,

when the *grande dame* raises her dress top.
Nipples fat, breasts full, she suckles,
before gaping eyes and mouths, the whole
infant brood; yet still the white flow as from
a hidden spring. Enough to fill earthenware
pitchers, bowls, form pools in sandy soil.

Jael

"Then Jael . . . took a hammer in her hand . . .
and smote the pin into (Sisera's) temples,
and it pierced through into the ground . . .
so he swooned and died." Judges, 4

She brought him milk and a bowl of curd,
undressed and washed him, covered
his nakedness with a leopard rug.
Sisera aspired on wafts of myrrh and spikenard,
forgot about his iron chariots,
nine hundred strong, routed this day
by the Hebrew witch, Deborah.
Moonlight
beaming in its press of gold, he dreamed
of a woman spider-queen, arching her back
with the grace of a gazelle, weaving
her precious thighs, everywhere spreading
a glutinous web of silk.
First his hands,
then feet stuck in a myriad of swirls.
She drew close, tresses flowing sumptuously,
lips poised with a black widow dose of bliss

when the tent-pin struck.

Samson

*". . . and God divided the light
from the darkness." Genesis 1:4*

He lay on the soft curve
and swell of her lap
as at the bottom
of a hill. Easier

to have wrestled
the lion than her taunts,
till the words, never
before spoken, had trickled

out. He lay, hair flowing
freely from a Nazirite's
vow, as close to the womb
as he could be

in her lap where night
came. Even the name,
Delilah, from *layelah,*
which means night.

The razor that would
stroke him like a baby,
just a caress. Around
his waist, Eden's

snakes undulate, turn
into the harlot
of Gaza's legs. Giddy
with the pleasure of that.

When he pushed against
the pillars of the temple,
at the jeers and laughter,
the priests with their pagan

rites, the geomorphic
fissures of betrayal—
a shaking. Then the cata-
clysm of stone and rock,

the huge bronze statue
of Dagon too, half fish,
half human, hurtling
down. Three thousand screaming

people, even the boy
who'd led him
to the pillars, crushed.
The image before death:

how the soldiers
had come to him barely
awakened on her lap,
come with knives for the eyes

as he lay, seven locks
of hair, jet black,
freshly scattered on the rug,
an aureole around them.

Webs

Moths

The he-moths and she-moths move to the flame
precipitously. Around and around
in a bizarre, phantasmagoric game,
transfixed by the light, no breath, not a sound,
only scary repetitive passes
impelling an arthropodous flier,
that, and the corrosive smell of gases
burning. An inferno. If desire
singes the wing-tips, there is still no hold.
The heart may protest but does not delay
this returning,
                    headstrong and uncontrolled—
a devolution.
                    No place to rest, no way
back through the chrysalis. A tidal moon:
all rationality is illusion.

What Other Couples Want To Know

Is the creature a couple?
Does it have a pair of heads, four arms,
use the royal "we"?
Like Narcissus, stare
at itself in the water?

Does it defend itself
with "shoulds" and "shouldn'ts,"
gush over babies?
Let both halves be dull,

like parsnip and squash,
this Mister and Missus together,
upon seeing another like itself, it is . . .
oh so friendly. Is the creature
a couple? If not,

and not at a tender age,
too young to know better,
or with an excuse—
death or divorce—it turns

away. Awkward, ambling along,
it purports to think as one: has four eyes,
four legs, is bored with both halves
of itself but will never admit it.
Is the creature a couple?

Pas De Deux

When Marguerite danced around Faust,
supple and girlish, a swirl in the white
silk dress, a blush on her cheeks,

caught him in the worm of her smell—
a sachet blend of herbs, flowers—,
with the hook, Mephisto, grinning

like a pitchman at some sideshow
rubes. When she flashed eyes shimmering
their moonlit lakes, and in the surrounding

brush, a savant, wrinkled, hungry
for communion,
                        touched him where God
was not, he signed the contract on the spot.

Audrey Rose

Little Ivy from the dark coils
beyond consciousness
remembers. Fingers pressed
to the apartment window,
she screams. They burn badly,
need ointment and bandages.
So in Europe, Eastertime,
a woman yearly bleeds
from her wrists and ankles
at the same spots where Christ
was rigged to the Cross
like a sail on the mizzenmast.
Ivy is torn by her earlier
incarnation, if such things be.
She's got five year old Audrey
in her, fingers eternally clawing
at the window casket lid
from within the crashed car, the cry—
like Munch's lady's, with sinuous
lines of oil and tempera horror,
on the twilight bridge
while flames lick and spoil.

Herr Wolf

They buy the cutest mobile
for the crib, a mouse whose tail
you can wind for song—*see how they run,*
they all ran after the farmer's wife,
she cut off . . . There's a smile
on everyone's face. The father, Alois.
Mama Klara. A countdown the first few
months to the magic nine. Is it moving about?
Drifting, swimming, recapitulating
all of evolution—thump! thump!—
in this period before birth.
He comes out
with an undescended testicle, opens
his mouth for a choleric wail. A black
hole, *Das Loch*—he will suck in matter:
trees, branches, shoes, pants, lovers
still unborn—Mimi Reiter, Geli Raubal,
Eva Braun—, gold teeth, gypsies, Jews, Slavs.
Will spit out bones from the Ringstrasse in Vienna
to Warsaw, Dachau, Bucharest, Belzec,
Paris, Kiev.
Oh love, you mocking sun
from this moment: Klara, who mourned
her dead children—diphtheria had strangled them—
was compulsively cleaning in the kitchen.
Alois slipped behind, plastered a kiss
on her neck. Minutes later in bed,
to a clock ticking and the smell of eiderdown,
he pumped sperm into her, hundreds of millions.
They wiggled through the vagina, uterus,
some up the Fallopian tubes. Only *one*
made it to fertilize—call that fate—the egg.

Narcissus And The Aquarium

from the Immaculate Collection *video*

She sits on a chair in a black bustier,
see-through black net stockings,
black gloves, a black wig. Takes it off.
Hmmmm. Blond. Gets up and dances.
Sings: "My desire burning inside me . . .
open your heart . . ." And it does.
Lithe, voluptuous with sin-
uous legs. There's a patron in each cubicle;
a man plays Toulouse-Lautrec,
sketching furiously with a pen. Another
loosens his tie.
                    The clock has stopped
at One. Wheeew. Smoking. Hotter than
hot. Lonely men: she's surrounded
by them, though from behind
glass partitions, each in his own way,
longing . . . An aquarium of the mind;
and what a wish she is, slippery
with love, try to hang on: to these
dreamy-eyed voyeurs, sad sacks, studs.
"I hold the lock," she croons
from an empty stage, "you hold
the key."
          Erotic nightscape. Land like Oz,
bathed in a blue-white light. She plays
with the chair now, stretching, posing
beside it; moves a few steps away,
wizard-cum-succubus, lips pursed red,
gold cones glittering on her breasts;
returns, brushing for an instant the rattan-like

back: it's the only prop on the stage.
I hold the lock the lock the lock . . .
And all of those eyes drawn, *desire burning*
inside . . . She struts
                                        across the floor, drags
her prop—armless—by its back. Twirls it
to the swell of the music. Sits facing
the back, straddles that chair! Mask
after mask—Madonna, Dietrich, Delilah,
the Whore of Babylon . . . Nothing about this
is real. The floor, so polished, it has the sheen
of a mirror. She pitches downward
to lie on it, her legs rising to greet—
perfect, the shape of them. Smiling like Narcissus,
admirer of her body there; then upward
at herself. From glass everywhere. In the blaze of eyes . . .

Anniversary

A missing chamber in the heart, cyanic
lips. The eyes alone plead.

She would've been in blue jeans and sixteen
this month, giggling on the telephone, her new

umbilical cord. When they took her home—
a heart transplant soon, dangled

like a gold fob-watch for a cat's paw—,
they washed her, nursed her in the crib,

this haggard little doll, shallowly breathing
in and out. Four weeks of changing diapers.

For what? After the funeral service,
his wife's scream *you don't care* sawed through

him, spitting off shavings, chips. She knew
how to squeeze hurt from the sponge

to the last drop. And did! Jennifer: his first.
A miracle gone bad, like milk that sits

for a month, curdles. Now every January,
even when he doesn't remember, when the wind

swirls white ghosts over dried grasses, weeds,
there's a missing chamber in the heart.

Vision

A welter of color inside—diuretics,
tranquilizers, tetracycline—the chassid's

pillbox seems made for a child to play with.
The capsules, like marbles to roll, candies

to suck. He also uses insulin, buys it
in bulk with a gross of needles. All this

to survive the body's storms—rain slashing
like knives, snow swirling in hyperborean blasts.

He'd will an end, were there a passing through
for sure, some delectable houri, waiting

even for a Jew. *Shalom!* she'd say, eternally ready
with the hips. When his virtue slips, he studies

Torah, Talmud. Judah Ben Tema, Abtalyon, Hillel
are friends. So is lithium. He seeds the clouds

with it. His libido rises, and the Baal Shem Tov,
guru from an age of werewolves, warlocks dances

once again in the Carpathian Mountains, drawing
souls together. *Likut nitzotzot:* the in-gathering

of dispersed sparks. *Come!* He beckons from
across centuries, the pockets of his black vesture

filled with holy miracles. Then, like a presti-
digitator, he's gone. In a test-hospital, aka/gehenna

the man with the pillbox screeches. Figures
in white float by him with words, potions, needles.

His eyes shut defensively, right arm, left
poked, prodded. Elusive are the arteries to God.

The Man Who Said No

for Yihya Avraham who kept his vow

For forty-four years he said: "No."
The paper describes how he died
in an Israeli prison,
a cerebral hemorrhage.
                                        His wife's plea,
"let me go," consent needed
for a religious divorce:
had it been love that drove him?
Or family?—
he had two daughters.
He was called, threatened, cajoled.
                                                    Later,
they passed a law that could put him
in prison. Still he said: "No."
They enforced the law. The sun waxed hot
and cold; he rarely saw it;
friends died; years passed. Always
the same offer: we'll let you out if . . .
Somehow he resisted.
                                        He seemed no longer
human. His wife howled: "From jail,
he should only go to his grave."
He filled with bile:
Some things should be freely given,
not this charade of law.
                                        Suspicious,
afraid to affix his name to anything.
"It's a trick," he thought, shaking his head
when they came with a piece of paper
for him to sign. It was for a canteen allowance.

Sign if you want a doctor: No.
Sign if you want visitor's privileges: No.
His eyes went wild.
                    There was no trick;
some papers you have to sign.
He refused to die, hung on . . .
How could they do this to anyone?
At the end in a dream they called him
senile. Under the chupa there,
stepping on the glass he knew was his life.
Shattered. A woman before him,
dressed in white like an angel.
She was death. And his. And beautiful.

Beasts, Reptiles, Snakes

"I'll be judge, I'll be jury," said
cunning old Fury; I'll try the whole
cause and condemn you to death."
Lewis Carroll, from
Alice's Adventures In Wonderland

Let a woman
splatter a man
with acid, cut him
with a broken bottle,
mutilate him with a knife,
poison shoot burn

him to ashes,
as long as she mouths the requisite,
"I'd been battered, raped,"
and without more, feminists
will hop in cars
and drive

cross country in support,
decrying the evil of men:
"oh, they are beasts, reptiles, snakes."
The more genteel of them
may begin, "it's not that we like
male bashing, but . . ."

after which disclaimer,
they will, with relish, do no less;
others, brazen, flaunting
tee-shirts with a sausage
on the front, mock an engorged
but dismembered

male organ.
Let a woman take up an ax—
a weapon fit
but a bit crude—
and though she whacks, not Peter,
but Paula, her Mother, a crime strictly

between the gentler sex,
they will look for the man
behind it: the husband she was unable
to leave, the father who had beaten her,
the brother who committed incest,
remembered for the first time

thirty years later, only
in therapy. "Free her!" they'll demand
as if *she* were the victim.
They'll want to fete her, put her
on talk shows—Donahue, Geraldo, Oprah.
And does that pouch nestled between

the voluptuous swell of her breasts
contain the ashes
of an erstwhile lover?
Tongues will cluck
at the effrontery of the warning there
to beasts reptiles snakes.

Ballade To Fanny Grummer

from Thaddeus, an admirer still

What didn't she call me—*dunce, idiot,*
baboon—whereupon her hand went back,
administered, before I could react,
a slap. She loosed a tooth, cut me no slack,
arms akimbo, an unnatural croak
to her voice, "You'll be *sorry.*" I awoke
to that warning . . . Just three words, nothing more.
What had I done? I started to slink/stagger
off to the john with such dire visions: jail,
poverty, death. If you could know my horror.
O low is the plight of this white male!

Betwixt and between: prison . . . a figment
of a derriere. For make no mistake,
my life is on an erotic bent.
A figment? Try separating real from fake.
My job. The adverse action (I choke . . .
to say it): the leech-lawyer spits me out broke.
The others (so many hiss and whisper).
I suffer so. Wander the corridor . . .
He's an har-ass-er, they accuse. Evil!
And yet, I'd watched her. Enraptured, reached for her . . .
Was it low, the path of this white male?

Sexual harassment: what her ass meant
to me—firm, but there were curves as could break
the heart. Her jeans, shapeful Wranglers that want
nothing: have it all. It was with an ache
I'd followed—oh so discreetly—a coke
in hand, trembling. And did they not provoke,
those jouncy mounds? At the water cooler,
she hesitated, and then bent over . . .
I slowed to breathlessness—a tragical
impulse in the air—perfumed—took root there.
Low. The bottom. The dream. The white male.

A blur to the images, what I felt
and thought even as she began to slake
her thirst. I glanced right furtively, then left,
no one coming, the field was clear to make
an approach. And oh for the clever joke
when she turned, a choice bon mot. I took
a hard look, at what could send a churchgoer—
for a touch—*smiling* to Lucifer.
Nether orbs. A pair, gloriously full
and ripe. To ease the pain of a dreamer . . .
O low is the bliss of this white male!

Touch, did I say then?—although I didn't
think it, couldn't fathom it, be awake
to have acted thus; yet if the deed wasn't
in my head, could the fingers for their own sake
have moved to caress? But wait, I misspoke
of this: there was only a gentle stroke,
a passing gesture to that curvature.
Rotundities. Zounds! I took my measure—
a hand's worth—that even now I recall
in my shame, that fundament of pleasure.
Low. The bottom. The dream. The white male.

I sit on my duff. Let them lecture.
Words. What have I to say? A touch. Harasser?
Egad! My heart. Lust. The fantastical
love that I bear . . . Plunderer. Caricature.
O what can be lower than this white male?

Cyberspace Ballade

The computer came with a kink, minus
the software the box proclaimed pre-installed—
Windows, DOS, Quicken, Prodigy. No choice
but to take it back; still, I was enthralled
with the replacement—bright, glittering—hauled
it to the car, thinking: *"Now* I'll begin
to write that book." No inner voice recalled
me to sanity. O for the days when

with pencil or pen . . . Could it copy floppies!?
I tried toll free support, was put on hold
for two hours, unassuaged by a voice
that interrupted the muzak, reassured
that I should stay on the line. I'd grow old
waiting! To Hell with that! I slammed the phone
down. Unhooked the monstrosity. Lugged
it to the store, thinking: O for the days when

with pencil or pen . . . Ahhrr. I began to curse.
My back had gone out. Names on the boxes blurred—
Compaq, AT&T, Dell. And worse,
that *next* model I dragged home. One word
to describe it: "horrors." A popcorn sound.
"Could be hard disk problems," the technician
offered calmly. Was there somewhere a sword
to fall upon? O for the days when

with pencil or pen! In this Age of DOS,
RAM, microchip, and megabyte, I've a yen
to pick up a hammer. Shatter. Smash.
O for the days when with pencil or pen!

Poetry And The Wall

Whitman's followers consigned the forms to hell—
sonnets, ballades . . . "Wait," cried lovely
Kyrielle in a high-pitched voice, "I've got
something beautiful . . ." But she was swept
away with the rest. What was Kyrielle like?
Shapely in a ballerina's dress, she wove
a tapestry of quatrains as she swirled in graceful
arabesques. She fell in love then with Pantoum,
who liked to dance in a huge circle, repeating
himself every few lines as if she didn't hear.
Of course, she heard: she loved him, married him,
had two children—Roundel and Villanelle.
But a wall was built, crude, thick,
and it kept her and her family away.
This was the Age of the new elite; they took
the places of the old and held all the weapons,
intellectual cannons, tanks, bombs to obliterate . . .
They called it PC, "poetical correctness."
Kyrielle went to Montauk, New York to commune
with Whitman, who as a boy had hurled
poetry at the waves there. "Why have you made
us pariahs?" she asked at the beach.
"Whoever you are, now," she heard him say,
"I place my hand upon you, that you be my poem . . ."
(Or was that just the crash of the waves?
Pantoum is my poem, she was thinking:
one should be loyal to husbands)

". . . and the pismire is equally perfect,
and a grain of sand." Kyrielle flushed red,
clenched her fists at the word *pismire.*
She wanted to diss him now, or wish him
away. "Free verse is dead!" she shouted
at the surf, agitated, roiling. That was for Pantoum:
when she thought of him, or of Roundel
or Villanelle, she was beyond reason or rhyme.

Webs

Like wisps of morning fog
not burnt off, or festive
bunting on buttonbush,
lizard's tail. An odd patchwork
of directions in these spider
webs: slanted diagonal
vertical athwart in
meadow wetlands. We, who
have been stuck, hand here,
heart there, weave our lives beside
the like of these, spinning out
the fabric too, sometimes
invisible, not sure
if any of it can be
undone. Salvador Dali—
his limp clocks folded over
branches like slices
of cheese or linen to dry—
would've loved to paint all
of this. He, who understood
the timelessness in perfervid
phenomena, would've reached
for his palette, but now
instead of blood and maggot,
the fine silken strand.

Cosmic Law

Like Atoms Which Can Neither Be Created Nor Destroyed

In Kabbalistic lore, no more souls exist now
than at the beginning.
Adam and Eve may've had the luxury
of their own. Even more recently,
out of some thirty thousand citizens,
Athens produced Euripides, Aeschylus,
Sophocles, Socrates, Plato . . . That speaks
for itself. But today, too many people,
not enough souls. We share one,
that is, cohabit in it—if lucky, with scores of others;
if not, with hundreds. We need a new mathematics
to chart the effect of the grade of soul against
the mix of persons. To wit, if it were grade A,
and Idi Amin had cohabited
with Mother Theresa, discounting
the effect of the other soul mates—
let's assume there seventy neutral ciphers—
he would've boxed flowers,
and she, played with a pet crocodile—
though their personalities would've remained
generally true to form. Not so
with grades B and C: a lack of refinement,
especially in the latter, increasing the potential
for more fundamental trans-
ferences. Of course, it's important
who the key players are. With three or more
the interactions become complex.
If there are too many, the ethereal may dim
as from a circuit overload. Or worse!
And what will happen to the ciphers?
To understand this, is to explain history.

Shilluk Virgin

"The king . . . lay down with . . . a nubile virgin
at the door of the [execution] hut, was then walled up
and the couple were left without food, water, or fire . . . ."
from The Golden Bough, *by Sir James Frazier*

You have come, she says, acknowledging
the arrival of half-naked men,
spears and hippopotamus-hide shields in hand.
Coolly, it seems,
she follows them as if on her head
a jug of water
for the path back from the river. Her heart, though,
wild as the tom-toms that beat:
a dance de rigueur, ebony bodies, the huge fire.

The hut where the King waits
is like the part of oneself a lifetime of denying doesn't erase.
A vision from sleep: the hooded skull of a moon,
a green field—
not grass but snakes—and the dreaded *jal yath,*
who twists nails
into a carved image with high cheekbones, thin lips.
Her own.

They condemn her for what she hasn't done in this life.
As if being sealed in a tomb
to the howl of hyenas and a kudu horn
could make the crops grow, cattle healthy.
Only room for herself and the King. A softening
if he moves to her, that she should awaken
in the dark just this once, and, like the White Nile, overflow
before the journey to *Pa Jwok,*
where her mother, long dead from a huge black spitting
cobra, wraps herself
in a favorite blue cloth, starts to chant.

Sorceress

She chops off a snake's head, inserts
into the jaw a seed from the ramma plant.
Takes it to a grave seven days old—
no more, no less. Buries it there
with incantations and for three nights
of watering, until the ramma seedling
first appears. As she steps out of
her clothes, lies down with a cache
of the snake's fat to rub on the tender
shoots, she's just another shadow
in a topography of fallen tree, turned-over
earth. *Do not show fear,* she'd been told,
so that when a djinn in the form of a man
appears, she smiles hard as stone,
and when a giant snake—a djinn too—
comes at her, she stays as if this moonless
expanse of dust and night were totemic,
to be fought over. It slithers past . . .
Every day now, she returns to see
the thing through. Measures the growth
with an adept's eye. One foot, two,
three . . . four. In the shimmer of light
from a flooding moon, she disrobes
once more. Pulls up the leafy green . . .
Winds it as if it were a girdle, twice
around a slender waist, ready for wish
to transform it into snake—mamba,
gaboon viper, bushmaster, boomslang: venom
to semen, and, at her will, back again.

Ehrich Weiss, AKA Houdini

From the San Francisco Bridge,
hands and feet manacled, a seventy-five pound
iron ball chained to the ankle, he jumps,
flouting both sides of the coin:
the conventional strait-jacket of nine-
to-five dying, and what lies

beyond. And when he hits water—
as much a bullet as the one
the Great Wizard of the North, Anderson,
had fired pointblank at himself, caught
between the teeth—
                    gone are the beer halls,
dime museums, vaudeville fantasies
of yesterday. Present, what must be done
with muscles, perception, will, quickly,

no time or place for slipping. Fear
presses against the barricades. A lifetime
of self-discipline holds, for the moment.
They won't give, these handcuffs.
He thought he knew the right snap or pick
for all the models, dared the audiences
to choose.
            Barely a minute's passed. The hurting
lungs have strength yet. The iron ball drags
him deeper, as if some adducent matter from
the ocean floor were in it seeking home. Fish
drift by, stare uncomprehending at this novelty
of agony. He tries again.

                    There! Free at the hands!

Mama! What a ride!
And if she dies . . . .
His hands and feet tear at the ankle chain.
Darkness races up at him,
like the nightmare when he closes his eyes
he fronts always.

But she does die. And ritually
he will visit the grave at dawn and fifteen
minutes after midnight—the moment of her passing—
just as he'd gone to the graves, mostly magicians',
for years, with flowers to bless the tradition:
Frickel, Doebler, Pinetti, Robert-Houdin.
Only now he's weeping, reaches across

the gulf. Every other day, a visit to a new medium:
chairs float by; untouched accordions
play; spirit faces with ectoplasmic emanations.
Ehrich, they call with phony inflections.

He seeks within too—if technique,
honed to its end point, can trigger
psychic forces that create real magic,
then . . . . —swears to find
a way, even as he dreams of being nailed
into a box sent hurtling over Niagara Falls,

afterwards to appear mysteriously safe
on shore, or to die and insinuate himself
back. A first!—as when flush with exhilaration
and a fragile Voisin biplane,
he'd brought aviation to Australia years
before,
circled for five minutes high above
Digger's Rest, while his entourage cheered.

Carousel

Boy chases girl around
the pastel horses
on a carousel getting ready
to start when a woman
picks up a sawed-off rifle

and points it. If our existence,
as Berkeley has asserted,
is only in God's mind,
what does that say of rage
exploding like a shriek? Her truck

had just rammed a rental car.
Now she pulls the trigger
and Uwe-Wilhelm Rakebrand,
a German tourist and stranger,
gets a .30 caliber bullet

in the back. Kant sees bias
in the human mind: it's cause-inclined.
The woman, claiming inspiration
from the rap song "Gangsta Bitch,"
rasps: "What goes around

comes around." No longer
elusive, girl is caught
by boy, who gives her a kiss
an instant before Rakebrand expires
as if the two events are con-

nected. A strange God, Berkeley's!
For Hume, no point looking
for a cause: there is none!
Two youngsters on a carousel. A man
dead. We have to go from there.

Shoe Shine Man

You sit beside azaleas and forsythias,
addressing an attractive foot.
Ladies in sheer hose with flailing
skirts and briefcases click past.
All day long, every day, you are here—
a bundle of polishes, brushes, rags—
watching, waiting.
                                        She smiles at the reflec-
tion of her face in pumps, rises
from your sidewalk stool, dazzling
in silk mauve chemise and the scent
of soft perfume. She asks: *How long
are you here in the street?* You respond
beatifically: *All day! All night!*
                                                        Later,
curled in a plush quilt,
she dreams of Christ incarnated as a shiner,
polishing souls as well as shoes
on the corner of Twentieth and K.
You recline on a favorite sewer grating
with phthisic cough, shabby gaberdine coverlet.

Cosmic Law

"The rule is jam tomorrow, and jam
yesterday—but never jam today."
Lewis Carroll from Through The Looking Glass

Then we meet, not at a singles bar,
but one for salads: *Roy Rogers*'.
She's cute, sassy, has a smile
like a pixie. *So much for cosmic law,*
I chortle, preparing
a *modus operandi* for the seduction
of toothsome fillies.
I, being highbrow
and concomitantly romantic, court her
at the race track.
Alas, in the Fifth
Dork's Peter and *Su The Master* are nipped
at the wire. I feel
apoplectic, tremble that the thirteen
bills she's just lost, a bad number at that,
on top of the difference in age,
which is even greater,
will no doubt scratch us from some higher card.
In the parking lot, I gamble—
nothing ventured, nothing . . .—with a kiss,
come away like a leprechaun,
heels clicking.
At the Hunan Palace
the next week, a different plaint:
religion. Will she want me when she knows?
I slip it out

like a secret missive between egg rolls and
the very *unkosher* moo shi pork.
Under the table,
her high heel shoe slides
off and on my right calf I feel
a toe.
The flush on her cheek's
like the sunrise everyone should see,
even at 6 A.M.
Today, I go to the library,
read about: the Egyptian pyramids;
Hanging Gardens of Babylon; Statue of Zeus;
Colossus of Rhodes; Temple of Artemis;
Mausoleum at Halicarnassus; Lighthouse at
Alexandria,
waiting for the other shoe to
drop.

Leaf And Tree

At what point does a leaf see its green start to fade?
At what point does the sun seem less pure?
The air more compelling?
The mottled edge of brown start to fray the edges?
Although the others see the same to differing degrees,
It's still a lonely thing.
They speak in hushed whispers of the time growing short,
Of the cold getting worse.
Even late in the change away from summer,
The sun may be just right, the air so fine,
They forget,
Almost.
At what point does a leaf see itself going faster?
Turn to neighbors who smile sympathies,
But then turn away as if to ignore unpleasantries?
At what point does the leaf confront the tree
About the inequities involved?
Before the long
Fall.

The Train

We are not a stranger to the refrain
"All aboard." There is the promise of snow
about. The station master calls again

in a shout. The train hisses and winds blow.
We are not unfamiliar with the dream.
The station master wanders to and fro,

recycling humanity in a stream
toward the gleaming coaches. Within sight
engine vibrations are expending steam.

It is ready. Even the station light
has brightened, as if the revolving door
will soon perform its magic act. The night

sky lowers with snow, and as before,
suitcases in hand, we are still unsure.

Simulation

The car moves along the roller coaster track
on a motion picture screen
inside a carriage that rooted
to a pivot rotates
first left—synchronization
is the watchword—then upward and right
to match the video twists,
till squeamish
at the top we level out for the sheer
drop, join
in a welter of canned
screaming all the way
down the monster's
belly.
        Later, we try a less primitive
mechanism. Had signed divers waivers,
given childhood photos, talked
about ourselves to analysts *ad nauseam.*
The barker's cry: "experience life"
impels the last stragglers forward.
Electrodes are hooked to bodies, heads.
Then images start up. We all have our own
theater. So thus we traverse from the womb
to sex even. The wires simulate
it happening—so good, oh god—
on the screen. We think:
this is the best trip since . . .
                                        till the next
experience—each has its own peculiar biochemical
configuration—blows the circuits.

When the celluloid image, a bit more grey
than you but recognizable, reaches for a pill,
that stab is in *your* chest. Doctor, say it's not . . .
but it is. You learn to live with, displace. A new-found
friend: affection blooms. Until plunging from that height
to the bottom, so distant, terror
finally easing into darkness.

We get up. Wobbly
a bit in the legs. The whole experience in only
seventy years. It's unreal, someone says. We scatter.

The Tower

"Unhood the Hawks! The roar
Of universes crashing into War!"
Aleister Crowley from The Book Of Thoth

Flames. The mouth of the beast.
The crumbling Tower. The Eye.
Alone on a hill. Blasted.
The untenable lie.

Annihilation. Dis,
god of the dead, belching
the flames. *Guernica*-like,
but no horses. Falling . . .

Mouths twisted; screams that want
to . . . can't. This is the realm
of fallacy, or is
it phallus? Overwhelm-

ing delusion. The vision
is yellow, black, red.
The Eye of Horus, watching,
floats, disembodied

takes everything in:
all manifestation,
from that flash of lightning
at the Tower's crown

to this cataclysm—
brick, stone. . . ephemeral,
the bodies, transforming—
one moment, corporeal

suffering; and the next,
mere geometrical
shapes, distorted beyond
recognition, hurtle

to an abyss: awareness,
unblinking like a sun,
through it all, no matter
how dark the confusion

of want, horror . . .

∞

The path
is *Peh,* Hebrew
letter/word meaning "mouth."
It takes us into

what is hidden. Orifice/
artifice, the cant
of speech. The lonely
garrison: call it

what you will. *Der Turm, La Tour,*
The Tower—a pyre
of lies, self, ego, sep-
arateness, to the fire

sure as truth, these dried leaves,
many layered, catching,
illuminate—as it
tumbles down. A burning

light through the windows.
And by the outermost
portal through a half-raised
grate: God's light for the lost.

∞

This is the Blasted Tower.
The Eye alone watches.
It's outside, this oval;
now moon-like, it catches

the scene on the hill with rays
unveiling: swaths of red
as with mortal, blood . . .
lamps shatter, a bed

heaves across the room,
walls collapse. No, worlds . . .
The sky pitches, reels.

∞

Unhood the hawks, birds

of prey! They take off, lunging
from the gloved fists, climb, soar,
blind to all but the call
of hunger. Their gyre,

hunger's, is War—hawk
after ravenous hawk.
More now, unhooded—
intemperate beak,

slashing talons—dart up
with a flutter. Each, a spark
till the heavens fill
ribbing the dark

night with the passion
of want. The need to break
out . . . No shelter in
that rubble of brick

and stone. To what new
dimension? Towerless
vistas: a place from before . . .
The sky, though, a mass,

moving, roiling . . . Cosmic
Eye that sees through the fall
to what's perfected,
nothingness, Mother of all.

The Mephisto Waltz

Around the grave, black is the color.
The earth flies back, coffin creaks open.
Bones, decaying flesh totter out.
Praise God! his wife cries out, falls
into his arms. Adult children stand
beside them. *Congratulations,* everyone says.
Retirement's not the thing. He takes up
lawyering, wins a big case; but his salary
drops. The kids have schoolwork problems.
Nothing to worry about, just like their ole Dad,
he hoops and hollers, chases Mom,
mesmerized by her indecently worn negligee.
The children dematerialize. He doesn't
miss them. At the wedding, his wife
is dressed in cotillion white. Solemn vows
punctuate his movement into bachelorhood.
Egad! Acne! A period of priapic concern,
loneliness, study. His comets are dreams.
He'd become a poet, grows smaller, half-heartedly
roughhouses with his brother—a little thug
not interested in Shakespeare, Marlowe.
He draws closer to Mother. Her body's a lure.
One minute he's sucking on a breast, the next
he's spanked. Finally, he's inside drifting in
amniotic fluid, thinking: *all the world's a stage,*
when the world blanks out. Her friends
console her. *He lived a good life,* they say.

Because He Didn't Ask For Directions

He was lost and found a yellow warbler
on the wrong path, saw a caterpillar
that wriggled through the grass not knowing

what one day it would be, wind blowing
in his face hard. He was lost and missed
the ferry at the time planned, crisscrossed

Oak Bluffs on Martha's Vineyard, sat down
in a café beside the woman
with pouf hair and an expansive look . . .

He said something light in the time it took
to quaff a beer. And she'd retell it
that night, but with her own inimit-

able slant, from which it took on
a strange life . . . He didn't ask direction,
somehow found his way back to the dock

and the ferry, while from out of the cloak
of the words he'd spoken, it was as if
a magus' rabbit had darted off,

become a sea gull rising, soaring . . .
Because he was a man without mooring,
he stumbled upon the tiny girl

on the deck (as the boat in a swirl
of motion headed back for Wood's Hole),
her face lit with a mischievous smile

(a potato chip held as lure over
the side), transfiguring to rapture
when a gull swooped down, half in play,

half in hunger, carried them both away.

Notes

PASS OVER

Patriarch

My father remained in Latvia for a number of years until his family, which had preceded him to America, could raise enough money to secure his passage. He was in his late twenties when he arrived at Ellis Island.

FLESH THAT WAS CHRYSALIS

Eden

Samael is the Prince of Gehenna, the fallen angel from whom the evil inclination originates.

Lilith

In Kabbalistic legend, Lilith's fall followed her refusal to lie beneath Adam in intercourse.

Flesh That Was Chrysalis

Enoch was the man who "walked with God, and he was not; for God took him." Gen. 5:24. He lived in the generation of evildoers in the time of the Deluge, and according to 3 Enoch of the Apocrypha, he was transformed as he ascended into heaven, and became Metatron, God's highest ministering angel. An "imago" is an insect in its final, sexually mature stage. It is also an idealized image of another person, or the self.

Isaac's Weaning Feast

The Talmud, B. Baba Metzia 87a, tells the story of ninety-year old Sarah playing wet nurse to all the children at Isaac's weaning feast. See *Gates To The Old City* by Raphael Patai, at p.192. The terebinth is a small tree of the Mediterranean that yields a resinous liquid.

WEBS

Audrey Rose

Edvard Munch's famous painting, *The Cry,* was completed in 1893 and hangs in the National Gallery, Oslo, Norway.

Herr Wolf

In his book, *The Psychopathic God: Adolf Hitler* (1977), p. 152, Robert G. L. Waite speculates on whether the abnormality of Adolf Hitler's genitalia contributed to his psychological abnormality. As to the title of the poem, Mr. Waite notes Hitler was fascinated with wolves. At the start of his political career he chose Herr Wolf as his pseudonym. He named his headquarters in France *Wolfsschlucht* (Wolf's Gulch). He named his headquarters in the Ukraine Werewolf. He called his SS "My pack of wolves."

Narcissus And The Aquarium

Based upon a viewing of the video, "Open Your Heart," from Madonna's *Immaculate Collection,* with acknowledgement to Camille Paglia's essay, "Madonna II: Venus Of The Radio Waves," in the book of essays entitled, *Sex, Art, And American Culture.*

Vision

The Baal Shem Tov ("Master of the Good Name") was the Eighteenth century founder of Chassidism, Israel ben Eliezer. The Baal Shem Tov's teaching is filled with parables and maxims, such as: "To pull another out of the mud, man must step into the mud himself."

The Man Who Said No

The impetus for the poem was a December 6, 1994, story in *The Washington Times*, titled "Stubborn man keeps his marriage vow," which tells of the life and death two days earlier of Yihya Avraham, a man jailed in Israel since 1962 for refusing to agree to a divorce.

Beasts, Reptiles, Snakes

The story of Lorena Bobbitt, who cut off her husband's penis, captured the country's interest in the fall of 1993. A jury found her not guilty by reason of insanity. The case, and the different views of the sexes, reflected an era of increasing gender tensions.

COSMIC LAW

Like Atoms Which Can Neither Be Created Nor Destroyed

After he deposed Ugandan President Milton Obote in 1971, Colonel Idi Amin expelled 40,000 East Indians and slaughtered at least 300,000 Ugandans, some of whom were alleged to have been fed to the crocodiles. Amin was deposed and fled the country in 1979.

Shilluk Virgin

The entombing of a virgin with the King who has lost his powers, i.e., evidence of the departure from his body of the divine spirit of Nyakang, appears in *The New Golden Bough* (New Mentor Library, Abridged Mentor Ed., 1959, pp. 275-276) by Sir James Frazier. The spirit of Nyakang entered the body of each King, and leaves it for a successor at an appropriate time. The *jal yath* is a witch doctor, and *Pa Jwok*, the name of the afterworld.

The Tower

The poem is based upon the tarot card, "The Tower," from the "Aleister Crowley Thoth Tarot" deck. This card has a divinatory meaning of calamity or adversity, but may involve insight, or perception of truth. The hawks in the epigraph symbolize vision as well as the energy that comes from a martial spirit, two aspects necessary for achieving higher states of consciousness. Aleister Crowley in *The Book Of Thoth,* (U.S. Game Systems, Inc. 1988 reprint, originally published in 1944), p. 108, indicates that to understand one aspect of the card, it is necessary to appreciate the Yoga doctrine of Southern India, involving the cult of Shiva. That doctrine provides that: "[T]he ultimate reality (which is perfection) is Nothingness. Hence all manifestations, however glorious, however delightful, are stains. To obtain perfection, all existing things must be annihilated. The destruction of the garrison may therefore be taken to mean their emancipation."

Horus, an Egyptian god, Harpocrates (literally meaning Horus the child), is also written as Hru, and is known as the "Great Angel of the Tarot." See Robert Wang, *Qabalistic Tarot*, (Samuel Weiser, Inc. 1983), p. 248. In legend, Horus, in seeking to avenge the death of his father Isis, has his right eye torn out by his father's murderer, Set, the god of the earth. Hence, the "Eye of Horus," not "Eyes," in the poem.

In Qabalistic tarot (which the Crowley deck follows), there are ten sephiroth (emanations). They correspond to the ten branches on the Jewish Kabbalistic tree of life. The Tower card is located between two of the sephiroth—Hod (Splendor) and Netzach (Victory). The path between the two is identified by the Hebrew letter Peh, meaning "mouth."

About the Author

Mel Belin was born in 1948 in Hazleton, Pennsylvania. He has a B.A. in Psychology from Dartmouth College and a J.D. in Law from George Washington University Law School. He is currently an attorney at the Department of Housing and Urban Development. He resides in Arlington, Virginia.

A Jenny McKean Moore fellow in creative writing at George Washington University, he has presented his poetry in numerous venues throughout the Washington, D.C. area, from Miller's Cabin and the Rock Creek gallery in the District, to a host of other urban locales—synagogue, library, bookstore, café, cable television, government agency, etc. His poems have been published in literary journals and magazines nationwide.

About the Artist

Noi Volkov was born in Agapovka, Russia. He is a graduate of the Odessa Grekov Art College and the Leningrad Muchina Institute. His work has been exhibited in France, Italy, Russia, and the United States where he now makes his home. His work is collected in the National Museum of Ceramics, Kiev; the National Museum of Ceramics, Baltimore, Maryland; Museum of Contemporary Russian Art, Jersey City, New Jersey; Zimmerli Art Museum, Rutgers University, New Brunswick, New Jersey; and the Cremona Foundation, Mechanicsville, Maryland.

About the Capitol Collection

The Capital Collection is a signature by the Word Works which features excellence in poetry from authors in the Greater Washington, DC area. The hallmark of this collection is that each book selected is financially supported by advance book sales and community contributions. The author also agrees to work with the press to promote the Capital Collection books, support other activities of the Word Works, and increase public interest in poetry. All inquiries must include a self-addressed stamped envelope.

The following individuals and organizations have contributed to the Capital Collection to make this book possible:

Patrons:
Donald A. Franck
James Hopkins
Miles David Moore
Hilary Tham
Ronnie & Abbot Wainwright

Donors:
Susan Absher
Mark L. Arnold
Roberta Beary
Reesa & Dan Belin
Cliff Bernier
Gregory Bolton
Mr. & Mrs. David R. Cooper
Lisa Kosow
Hugh Lutz
Judith McCombs
Daniel Meijer
Lenny Lianne Resch

Friends:
Barri Armitage
Grace Cavalieri
Monica Jordan
Ken Markison
Fay Picardi
Robert Sargent

Special thanks to the anonymous patrons, donors, and friends who also supported this book.

About the Word Works

The Word Works, a nonprofit literary organization, publishes contemporary poetry in collector's editions. Since 1981, the organization has sponsored the Washington Prize, an award of $1,000 to a living American poet. Each summer, Word Works presents free poetry programs at the Joaquin Miller Cabin in Washington, DC's Rock Creek Park. Annually, two high school students debut at the Miller Cabin Series as winners of the Young Poets Competition.

Since Word Works was founded in 1974, programs have included: "In the Shadow of the Capitol," a symposium and archival project on the African-American intellectual community in segregated Washington, DC; the Gunston Arts Center Poetry Series (including Ai, Carolyn Forché, Stanley Kunitz, Linda Pastan, among others); the Poet-Editor panel discussions at the Bethesda Writer's Center (including John Hollander, Maurice English, Anthony Hecht, Josephine Jacobsen, among others); Poet's Jam, a multi-arts program series featuring poetry in performance; a poetry workshop at the Center for Creative Non-Violence (CCNV) shelter, and the Writers' Retreat workshops and readings in Tuscany. In 1997 the Word Works began distributing chapbooks by Mica Press (Ft. Collins, Colorado) under a cooperative agreement.

Past grants have been awarded by the National Endowment for the Arts, the National Endowment for the Humanities, the DC Commission on the Arts and Humanities, the Witter Bynner Foundation, and others, including many generous private patrons.

Word Works has an archive of artistic and administrative materials in the Washington Writing Archive housed in the George Washington University Gelman Library.

Please enclose a self-addressed stamped envelope with all inquiries. Find out more about the Word Works at

http://www.writer.org/wordwork/wordwrk1.htm

Other available Word Works books:

Karren L. Alenier, **Wandering on the Outside**
Karren L. Alenier, ed., **Whose Woods These Are**
Karren L. Alenier, Hilary Tham, Miles David Moore, eds.,
Winners: A Retrospective of the Washington Prize
J. H. Beall, **Hickey, The Days...**
Nathalie F. Anderson, **Following Fred Astaire***
* John Bradley, **Love-In-Idleness**
Christopher Bursk, ed., **Cool Fire**
Grace Cavalieri, **Pinecrest Rest Haven** (Capital Collection)
Shirley Cochrane, **Family and Other Strangers**
Moshe Dor, Barbara Goldberg, and
Giora Leshem, eds. **The Stones Remember**
Harrison Fisher, **Curtains for You**
Isaac Goldberg, **Solomon Ibn Gabirol: A Bibliography of his Poems in Translation** (International Editions)
* Linda Lee Harper, **Toward Desire**
* Ann Rae Jonas, **A Diamond Is Hard But Not Tough**
Vladimir Levchev, **Black Book of the Endangered Species** (International Editions)
James McEuen, **Snake Country** (Capital Collection)
* Elaine Magarrell, **Blameless Lives**
* Fred Marchant, **Tipping Point**
* Barbara Moore, **Farewell to the Body**
Miles David Moore, **The Bears of Paris** (Capital Collection)
Betty Parry, ed., **The Unicorn and the Garden**
* Jay Rogoff, **The Cutoff**
Robert Sargent, **Aspects of a Southern Story**
Robert Sargent, **Woman From Memphis**
M.A. Schaffner, **The Good Opinion of Squirrels** (Capital Collection)
* Enid Shomer, **Stalking the Florida Panther**
Hilary Tham, **Bad Names for Women** (Capital Collection)
* Nancy White, **Sun, Moon, Salt**
* George Young, **Spinoza's Mouse**

* Washington Prize winners

Requests for our brochure and other information must be accompanied by a self-addressed stamped envelope.